8906

D0753434

DATE DUE

8906

EGYPT
the culture

Arlene Moscovitch

A Bobbie Kalman Book

The Lands, Peoples, and Cultures Series

 Crabtree Publishing Company
www.crabtreebooks.com

The Lands, Peoples, and Cultures Series
Created by Bobbie Kalman

Coordinating editor
Ellen Rodger
Proofreader: Adrianna Morganelli

Project development
First Folio Resource Group, Inc.

Pauline Beggs
Tom Dart
Kathryn Lane
Debbie Smith
Joyce Funamoto
Robyn Craig

Design
David Vereschagin/Quadrat Communications

Revisions and updates
Plan B Book Packagers
Redbud Editorial

Special thanks to
Sally Abuseif, Prof. Dr. Ahmed ElSherbini, Consul,
Bureau of Cultural and Education Affairs of Egypt;
Dr. N. B. Millet, Senior Curator, Egyptian Section,
Royal Ontario Museum, André L. Potvin, Ms. Elham
Yassin

Photographs
Art Resource, NY: p. 17 (top); Brian Brake/Photo
Researchers: p. 12, p. 16 (top), p. 19 (both), p. 21
(top); Corbis/Nathan Benn: p. 10 (bottom);
Corbis/Bettmann: p. 14 (top); Corbis/UPI-Bettmann:
p. 15 (bottom); Corbis/Hulton-Deutsch Collection:
p. 11 (top); Corbis/The Purcell Team: p. 14 (bottom); Marc Crabtree:
p. 4 (top), p. 20 (right), p. 22 (both), p. 25 (middle), p. 26, p. 27 (top);
Peter Crabtree: p. 6, p. 23 (bottom); Giraudon/Art Resource, NY: p. 20
(bottom); George Holton/Photo Researchers: p. 24; Faruq Ibrahim:
p. 25 (bottom); ©Wolfgang Kaehler, www.wkaehlerphoto.com: cover;
Vladimir Korostyshevskiy/Shutterstock, Inc.: p. 7; Erich Lessing/Art
Resource, NY: p. 9, p. 10 (top), p. 16 (bottom), p. 18 (top), p. 21
(bottom); courtesy of Marla Mallett: p. 27 (bottom); Fred
Maroon/Photo Researchers: p. 15 (top); Bill McKelvie/Shutterstock,
Inc., p. 1; Guy W. Midkiff: p. 23 (top); The Nobel Foundation: p. 29
(bottom); Richard T. Nowitz: p. 8 (top), p. 29 (top); Vova
Pomortzeff/Shutterstock, Inc.: p. 28; Carl Purcell: p. 8 (bottom);
Photograph courtesy of the Royal Ontario Museum, © ROM: p. 11
(bottom); Jose Antonio Sanchez/Shutterstock, Inc.: p.4-5; Scala/Art
Resource, NY: p. 13, p. 17; SEF/Art Resource, NY: p. 3; Werner
Forman/Art Resource, NY: p. 18 (bottom); Laura Zito/Photo
Researchers: p. 25 (top)

Every effort has been made to obtain the appropriate credit and full
copyright clearance for all images in this book. Any oversites, despite
Crabtree's greatest precautions, will be corrected in future editions.

Illustrations
William Kimber. A scarab, the sacred dung beetle of ancient Egypt,
appears at the head of each section. The Great Sphinx is shown on the
back cover.

Cover
Egypt has a long tradition of weaving fine cloth and colorful carpets.
This carpet maker weaves elegant patterns on a loom.

Title page
Egyptian temples often had columns with hieroglyphic inscriptions.

Library and Archives Canada Cataloguing in Publication

Moscovitch, Arlene, 1946-
    Egypt : the culture / Arlene Moscovitch.

(Lands, peoples, and cultures series)
Includes index.
ISBN 978-0-7787-9307-6 (bound)
ISBN 978-0-7787-9675-6 (pbk.)

    1. Egypt--Civilization--Juvenile literature. I. Title. II. Series.

DT70.M67 2007   j962   C2007-905713-6

Library of Congress Cataloging-in-Publication Data

Moscovitch, Arlene, 1946-
    Egypt the culture / Arlene Moscovitch.
      p. cm. -- (Lands, peoples, and cultures)
    Includes index.
    ISBN-13: 978-0-7787-9307-6 (rlb)
    ISBN-10: 0-7787-9307-9 (rlb)
    ISBN-13: 978-0-7787-9675-6 (pb)
    ISBN-10: 0-7787-9675-2 (pb)
    1. Egypt--Civilization--To 332 B.C.--Juvenile literature. 2. gypt--Civilization--1798---
Juvenile literature. I. Title.
    DT61.M69 2007
    962--dc22

                                                    2007037297

Crabtree Publishing Company
www.crabtreebooks.com   1-800-387-7650

Published in Canada
Crabtree Publishing
616 Welland Ave.
St. Catharines, ON
L2M 5V6

Published in the United States
Crabtree Publishing
PMB16A
350 Fifth Ave., Suite 3308
New York, NY 10118

Published in the United Kingdom
Crabtree Publishing
White Cross Mills
High Town, Lancaster
LA1 4XS

Published in Australia
Crabtree Publishing
386 Mt. Alexander Rd.
Ascot Vale (Melbourne)
VIC 3032

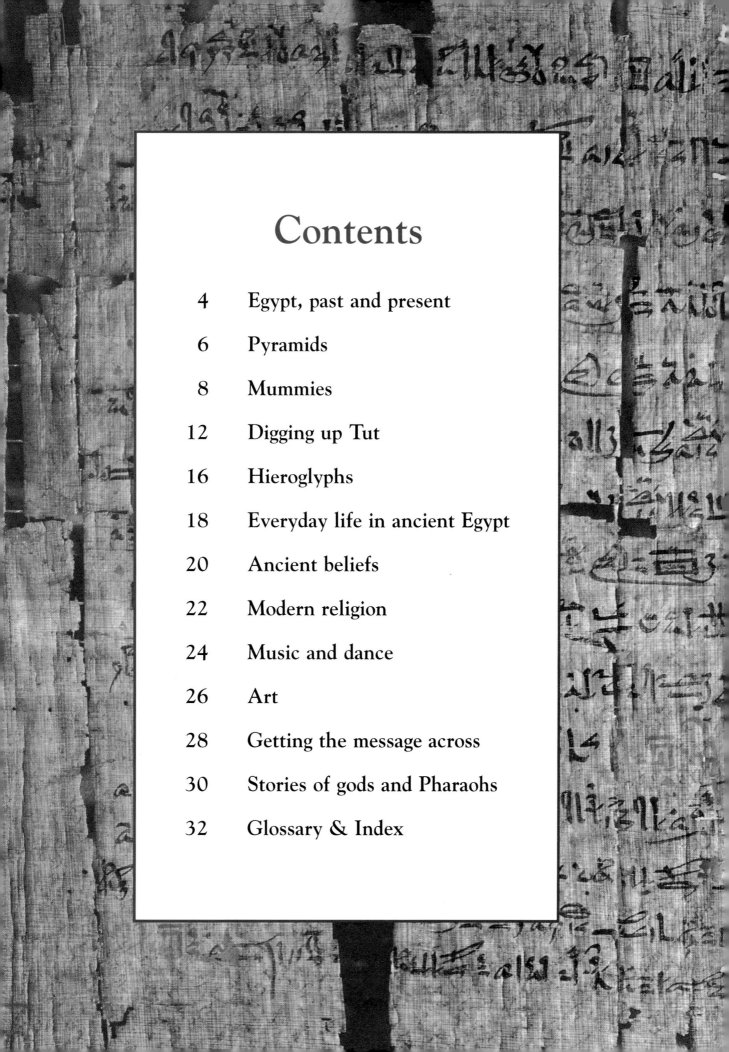

Contents

Egypt, past and present

(above) A very creative painter decorated this Nubian community center in southern Egypt.

Five thousand years ago, the ancient culture of Egypt flourished on the banks of the Nile River. For many centuries, powerful rulers, called **Pharaohs**, led the country. The people of ancient Egypt respected their leaders. Many of them helped construct buildings to honor their Pharaohs and the gods. Today, we can still see the result of the Egyptians' hard work. They left behind breathtaking **temples**, massive **pyramids**, beautiful wall paintings, and some of the world's first written records. Modern Egyptians are proud of their rich past, but they also value the culture created in more recent times. That culture mixes African, Asian, and European ideals. In Egypt today, the ancient and the modern are often combined.

(above) An image from a painted box found in the tomb of King Tutankahmun. In many ways, ancient Egyptian art continues to influence art created today.

(below) Modern housing near the pyramid at Giza. As Egypt's population grows, the country must find ways to house people without destroying ancient treasures.

Egypt's most famous **monuments** are the pyramids. These gigantic structures were built as burial places for the Pharaohs 4,500 years ago. Today, over 80 pyramids remain throughout Egypt. Most of them are found along the Nile River, from the middle of Egypt up to the capital city of Cairo, in the north.

The great Step Pyramid

The architect Imhotep built Egypt's first pyramid in about 2630 B.C. as a tomb for King Djoser. It is called the Step Pyramid because it has six stages, or levels. The Step Pyramid was like a giant staircase that the king could climb after he died. The staircase would lead him upwards to the Sun god, Re, one of the many gods that the ancient Egyptians **worshiped.**

The Step Pyramid is the oldest monument.

The pyramid's design

The later pyramids are shaped like enormous 3-D triangles pointing toward the sky. Some scholars think pyramids have this shape because of an ancient legend about how the world was formed. The Egyptians believed that in the beginning, there was an immense ocean called Nun. Out of this ocean, rose the first hill. The pyramids were built to remind people of this hill. The pyramids had false doors so that the spirit, or *ka*, of the Pharaoh buried inside could come and go as it pleased. Inside, long corridors led to secret rooms filled with furniture, weapons, jewels, and statues. These were placed in the tomb so the Pharaoh could use them in the **Afterlife**, where the ancient Egyptians believed that a person's body and soul existed after death. The pyramid contained a special room, or chamber, where the Pharaoh's body lay in its coffin.

Building the Great Pyramid of Cheops

The largest pyramid of all is the Great Pyramid of Cheops, at Giza. It is as tall as a 48-story building and covers an area the size of ten football fields. Building the Great Pyramid was an enormous task that took about 20 years. Thousands of craftspeople and laborers built this giant tomb. Every year, when the Nile River flooded the land for three months, the farmers could not grow crops. They were sent to help the other workers who were constructing the pyramid throughout the year. The workers dragged 2.5 million stone blocks up a ramp, one at a time. They placed the blocks one on top of the other. The stones fit together so well that they did not need any cement to hold them in place!

The ancient Egyptians were very skilled at preserving the bodies of the dead. They developed the art of making mummies because they wanted the people they loved to live forever in the Afterlife. For that to happen, the Egyptians believed the body and soul had to stay together after death.

Making a mummy

The Egyptians spent about 70 days **embalming**, or preserving, a body. First, the embalmers removed the brain through the nose with a special curved hook. Then, they removed the rest of the internal organs, except for the heart. Ancient Egyptians believed that the emotions and intelligence were stored in the heart. The dead would need their heart for a final test to decide if they could pass on to the Afterlife.

(above) Embalmers removed the lungs, liver, stomach, and intestines from the body. They wrapped the organs in strips of linen. Then, they stored each organ in a separate container, called a canopic jar, and buried the jars with the body.

(below) In this tomb painting, a priest wearing a mask of the jackal-headed god of the dead, Anubis, says the final prayers over a mummy.

Preserving the body

After the organs were removed, the body was covered with a solution of **natron**, a salty chemical. The natron dried out the body, so that it would not decay. It took 40 days for the body to dry out. Melted **resin**, or tree sap, was also poured over the mummy to preserve the skin. Finally, the embalmers stuffed the mummy's body with sand or wads of linen to give it shape. At last, the body was ready for the next step, the wrapping.

Wrapping the body

The embalmers wrapped the preserved body in strips of a cotton-like material called linen. Each arm, leg, finger, and toe was wrapped separately. A well wrapped mummy could be wound in up to 410 square meters (450 square yards) of linen. During the 15 days it took to finish the wrapping, priests recited special prayers over the body. After the wrapping, a funeral mask was placed over the dead person's face. Finally, the mummy was placed in a coffin or mummy case. These cases were made of richly decorated wood.

The Books of the Dead

The Books of the Dead were magic spells written on **papyrus** and placed on or near mummies. Egyptians believed that these spells would help dead people pass safely through the dangers of the **Underworld,** or Duat, on their way to the Afterlife. The Books of the Dead also contained a map to guide the dead on their journey. The final danger in the Underworld was the test in the Hall of the Two Truths. The dead had to prove to 42 judges that they were innocent of 42 terrible crimes. Then, their heart was weighed on a scale, with the heart in one pan and the feather of justice in the other. If they told the truth, the pans of the scale would balance and the dead would pass on to the Afterlife. The heart of evil people would upset the balance of the scales. Their soul perished and their heart was devoured by the monster Amut, who was part crocodile, part leopard, and part hippopotamus.

This ancient papyrus scroll shows gods weighing a dead woman's heart, as the bird-headed god, Thoth, records the results.

9

The famous hidden mummies

In 1881, a fabulous discovery was made. Gaston Maspero, an **Egyptologist**, or person who studies ancient Egypt, found 40 mummies in the depths of a mountainside tomb. They included many of Egypt's most famous Pharaohs and their royal families. Almost 20 years later, a second tomb was found nearby. It was filled with another 16 mummies. Originally, the Pharaohs were buried with gold and precious **amulets**, or magical charms, in their own tombs. Over the centuries, tomb robbers damaged many of the royal mummies while searching for these treasures. So, priests reburied the dead Pharaohs in two secret hiding places in the mountains at Deir el-Bahri, near Thebes, the ancient capital of Egypt. The Pharaohs lay there undisturbed for nearly 3,000 years. Today, the bodies of the ancient Pharaohs found in the mountainside lie in a special private room in the Egypt Museum in Cairo.

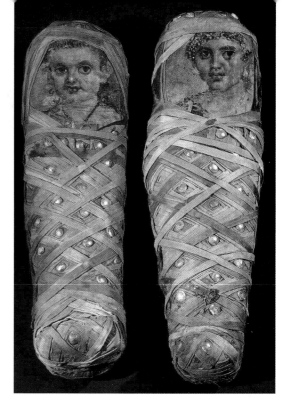

(above) Mummies changed over time. These mummies from 50 A.D. are painted with the portraits of the dead children wrapped inside.

(above) Ramses II, one of ancient Egypt's most powerful Pharaohs, was found at Deir el-Bahri. His embalmers were very skilled. Ramses II is in great shape considering he is over 3,000 years old!

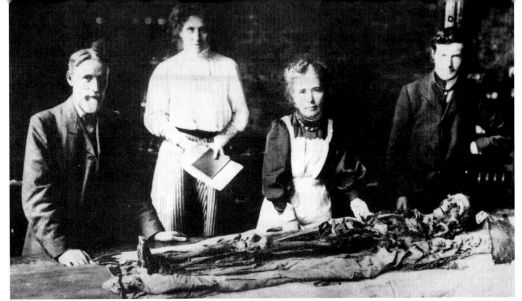

English scientists unwrap an Egyptian mummy in 1898. Mummies were sometimes bought from grave robbers.

Studying stolen mummies

Egyptian mummies are found in museums around the world. Many of those mummies were stolen from Egypt during the 1800s and early 1900s. Egyptologists brought the mummies back to their own countries where scientists and historians studied them. Mummies are a great record of the past because they can be used to determine what the ancient Egyptians ate and how long they lived. Recently, Egypt has tried to **repatriate** the mummies and other ancient treasures. In 2003, the mummy of Ramses I was returned to the Cairo museum. It had spent years in a museum in Niagara Falls, Canada, where no one knew it was a royal mummy!

High-tech research

In the past, when people wanted to study a mummy, they unwrapped it or cut through the many layers of cloth. This process damaged the fragile mummy. Today, scientists study a mummy using a number of high-tech tools, including computer imaging, radiocarbon dating, and a special x-ray called a CAT scan. The CAT scan lets them see parts of the body, including the skin and muscles, that they were not able to see using regular x-ray machines. From the CAT scans, they can produce a three-dimensional picture of the mummy. Scientists can then figure out what kind of diseases people suffered from thousands of years ago and how these diseases have changed over time. All of this research can help people today.

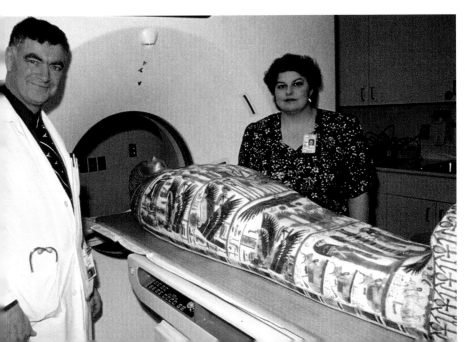

(left) The mummy of Djedmaatesankh has just had a CAT scan. Scientists figured out that she was a temple musician who probably died at 35 when a rotten tooth became badly infected.

 # Digging up Tut

Egyptologists learn about ancient Egypt by studying mummies, ancient architecture, and the everyday objects ancient people used, such as pottery, weapons, and musical instruments. Many of these objects have been found buried under sand, soil, or water, or inside tombs. One of the Egyptologists' greatest finds was the tomb of a king called Tutankhamun.

The great discovery

Howard Carter was a British Egyptologist who made an astonishing discovery in 1922. For five years, he had been digging in the Valley of the Kings where many Egyptian Pharaohs were buried. One day, he peered inside a dark tomb and was amazed at what he saw. He uncovered the tomb of the child king Tutankhamun.

The young Pharaoh

Tutankhamun became Pharaoh when he was eight or nine years old and died at the age of nineteen. Robbers had not discovered his tomb, so it was still full of treasures 3,200 years after his death. The king's mummy was wearing a mask of solid gold. His body lay inside three mummy cases, which fit one into the other. The smallest mummy case was 110 kilograms (242 pounds) of solid gold. Carter found statues, furniture, and jewelry. There was a painted box, stuffed with Tutankhamun's clothes, and a pair of his sandals. Carter worked very slowly and carefully to make sure that nothing would be lost or damaged. It took him almost ten years to examine all the priceless treasures inside Tutankhamun's tomb.

Curse of the Pharaoh

The opening of Tutankhamun's tomb was marked by coincidences that some people call the curse of the Pharaoh. Strange things happened to some of the people involved in the discovery. Lord Carnarvon of Britain, who paid for Howard Carter's expeditions to dig up the lost tomb, died in Cairo four months after the tomb was found. Other people connected with the discovery also died mysterious deaths. People began to wonder. Had Tutankhamun cursed the people who found him? Was he trying to tell them to leave his tomb untouched?

(below) Tutankhamun's neckband of the vulture goddess, Nekhbet, is very heavy. It is one of many pieces of jewelry found in his tomb.

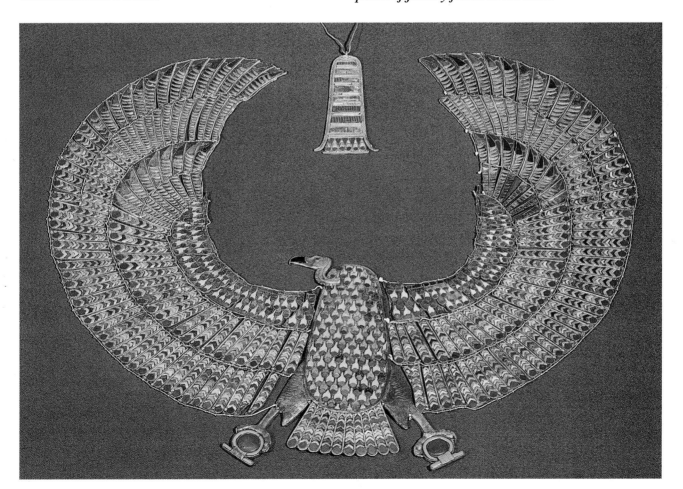

(opposite) Tutankhamun's famous death mask is made of solid gold. It covered the head of his mummified body.

The mystery remains

At the time, the curse of the Pharaoh made international newspaper headlines. Some people said that the many deaths were completely unrelated to the discovery. Lord Carnarvon died of an infected mosquito bite. Others who died were already sick before they came to Egypt to see the tomb. Still others, who had planned to come to Egypt, got sick and never even left their home country. Carter, who actually found Tutankhamun's mummy, lived for many years after his discovery. Still, many people are not convinced by these explanations and want to believe in some sort of ancient magic. The scale and worth of the tomb's discovery makes the story of a curse more exciting and appealing.

Damaged treasures

For thousands of years, Egypt's treasures were taken from their original resting places. Tomb robbers broke into the pyramids and stole many treasures that were sealed inside. Centuries later, people stripped off the smooth **limestone** that covered the pyramids and used it to decorate new buildings in Cairo. Travelers or **conquerors** from other lands took Egyptian objects back home with them. Many of them were not careful and they ruined many treasures.

Protecting the treasures of the past

Now, there is a law that all ancient objects found in Egypt must stay in Egypt. Most of them are preserved in museums. For example, the treasures of King Tutankhamun's tomb are in the Egypt Museum in Cairo. Tutankhamun's treasures have also traveled around the world in organized shows so that people in other countries can see them.

(above) In the 1890s, Egyptian guides hoisted tourists up the large stones of the pyramids. Once a popular tourist activity, it is now strictly forbidden to climb the ancient tombs.

(above) A tomb lies in shambles after being ransacked. Tomb robbers often pulled apart mummies hoping to find valuables wrapped inside the layers of cloth.

(above) Tutankhamun's gold throne is engraved with an image of the young king and his wife.

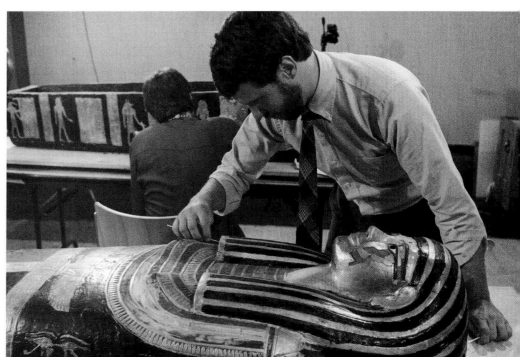

(right) A restorer carefully cleans a mummy case with a cotton swab.

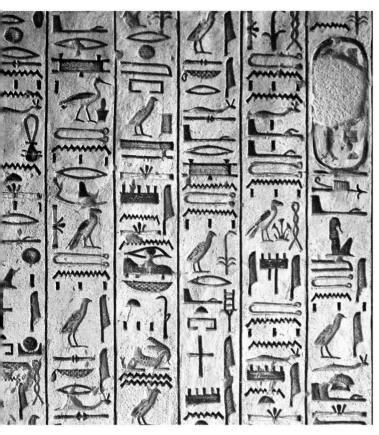

(above) It took great skill to carve and paint hieroglyphs as beautiful as these.

(below) Scribes measure a farmer's harvest. They write with reeds, which are hollow stalks from grass-like plants that grew along the Nile.

The Egyptians have the longest written history of any people in the world. Their ancient system of writing used words made with pictures instead of letters. Those symbols are called **hieroglyphs**. The ancient Egyptians wrote with hieroglyphs for 3,000 years.

Papyrus

Hieroglyphs were written on long scrolls of papyrus, a type of paper. Papyrus was made from papyrus plants, which grew along the banks of the Nile River. The Egyptians cut papyrus stems into strips and flattened them. Then, they soaked the strips in water and arranged them in layers. With a mallet, a type of hammer, they pounded the strips into sheets to make a writing surface. Papyrus was so light and easy to carry that the ancient Egyptians used it for 4,000 years. The ancient Greeks, Romans, and Phoenicians also wrote on papyrus, which the Egyptians sold to them in great quantities.

Scribe work and training

Many families in ancient Egypt encouraged their sons to become **scribes**, or professional writers. At the time, very few Egyptians could read or write, so skilled scribes were important in society. Scribes kept tax rolls, wrote prayers, and recorded judgments for the court. It took five years of study to learn how to write about 700 different hieroglyphs. Scribes also used hieratic and demotic writing, or scripts, for letters, stories, and business documents. These scripts were based on hieroglyphs and could be done quickly.

The Rosetta Stone

By the fifth century A.D., the people of Egypt were writing in the Greek language of their conquerors. They no longer understood what the hieroglyphs on their sacred tombs and temples meant. That changed after 1799, when a French soldier, who was building a fortress at Rosetta on the banks of the Nile, made an important discovery. His shovel hit a large slab of black stone. This stone had writing in three different scripts: hieroglyphs, demotic, and ancient Greek.

Cracking the code

For years, scholars in England and France tried to decode the Rosetta Stone. French scholar, Jean-François Champollion, finally figured it out in 1822. He used his knowledge of ancient Greek and the **Coptic** language still used in Egyptian churches to understand that the stone was a thank-you letter to Ptolemy, the Greek ruler of Egypt. Champollion first read the name Ptolemy in Greek. Then, he found the Egyptian hieroglyphs for the same word. From these beginnings, Champollion was able to figure out the meaning of all the hieroglyphs. His work helped the study of ancient Egypt.

(above) Hieroglyphs are carved at the top, demotic script appears in the middle, and ancient Greek is written at the bottom of the Rosetta Stone.

(below) The Books of the Dead are written on papyrus in hieroglyphs.

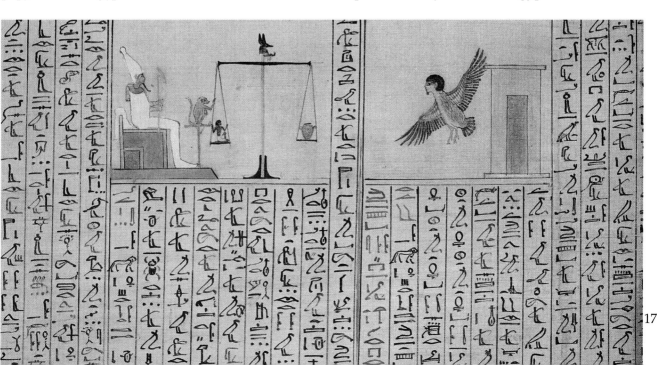

17

Everyday life in ancient Egypt

Famous tombs, like the pyramids, and amazing human remains, like the mummies, are a part of ancient Egypt. So are paintings, stories, and objects, such as toys, musical instruments, and pieces of jewelry. Together, these give us clues about what life was like for the people who lived during the time of the Pharaohs.

Fashion 3,000 years ago

The ancient Egyptians loved beauty and fashion. They spent a lot of time making sure they looked as good as possible. Their clothes were made of linen. Men wore long skirts knotted at the waist and women wore long dresses. Everyone wore sandals made of leather or reeds from the papyrus plant.

(right) A jewelry box filled with makeup containers and necklaces was found in a young girl's tomb. She lived almost 4,000 years ago.

(below) Young Egyptian women wear sweet lotus blossoms in their hair, perfumed cones of fat on their heads, and golden disk earrings.

Looking good

Both men and women often had short hair. For special occasions, they put on wigs of human hair that were held in place with beeswax. They smoothed oils and creams on their bodies to keep their skin soft. Teenagers even put on special pastes for their pimples! For makeup, the Egyptians used eye paints, rouge, and lipstick. To make the paints, they ground minerals and mixed them with water. Women and men both wore black eye paint, or **kohl**, which made their eyes look larger.

Homes

Most families in ancient times made their homes along the banks of the Nile River. Houses were built of mud bricks that were baked by the sun. Peasant families had small houses with a low rounded doorway. The houses of wealthy families had several floors, as well as a garden with a pool full of fish and flowers.

Family life

The ancient Egyptians usually married when they were teenagers. Daughters were taught at home and sons started going to school when they were seven years old. Boys became soldiers, scribes, craftsmen, and farmers. Girls became weavers, perfume makers, dancers, and musicians. Women also owned and ran farms, or became priestesses in the temples.

Toys and games

Children in ancient Egypt had something in common with children today. They loved to have fun. Young Egyptians played piggyback, leapfrog, and tug-of-war. Paintings and carvings from thousands of years ago show boys pretending to be soldiers and girls leaping to catch a ball in mid-air. Small children spun tops and pulled wooden toys, such as carved mice and horses on wheels. Some children even had animal toys with moving jaws and tails. Both children and adults loved to play board games. One of the most popular board games was *senet*. In this game, players moved their pieces around the thirty squares on the board. The winner was the first person to reach the kingdom of Osiris, the god of the Underworld.

(above) **In this ancient painting, a man hunts in a papyrus swamp.**

(left) **Queen Nefertari, the favorite wife of the powerful Pharaoh Ramses II, plays** senet **in a painting on the walls of her tomb.**

19

The ancient Egyptians were a deeply religious people who worshiped many gods and goddesses. The king of their gods was the Sun god, Re. The people also believed their Pharaoh was a god, as well as their ruler.

Gods and goddesses

Throughout the country, Egyptians built shrines, statues, and temples dedicated to their Pharaohs, gods, and goddesses. Many gods and goddesses were shown as being part human and part animal. For example, Anubis, the god who watched over the dead, had the head of a jackal. The Egyptians knew that jackals lurked in cemeteries. They thought that a jackal would know how to guide and protect the dead on their journey to the Afterlife.

(below) Towering columns line the Hypostyle Hall at the Temple of Horus in Edfu.

(above) Two Wedjat eyes peer from above Osiris, god of the Underworld.

(below) A jewelled scarab with wings pushes the orange disk of the sun in front of him.

Temples and priests

Each day, **priests** performed ceremonies to honor the gods and goddesses. Before the ceremonies, they cleansed and purified themselves in the temple's sacred lake. They also perfumed the air with incense and sprinkled holy water before the shrine to purify the space. Millions of visitors still visit these temples, only today they are tourists.

Amulets

Egyptians often wore amulets on necklaces or bracelets. They believed that the small figures of gods and animals would keep them safe from harm. They buried amulets with the dead to help them as they traveled to the Afterlife. The Wedjat eye was one of the most common amulets. People believed that the eye would protect them against evil. Even today, people in some parts of Egypt still paint the eye on the outside of their houses. Another favorite amulet was the scarab, or dung beetle. The beetle rolling a ball of dung between its front legs reminded Egyptians of the Sun god rolling the sun in the sky.

Horus holds an ankh, *a sign of life, and wears a sun disk above his hawk-shaped head. Hathor, the mother goddess, sits beside him.*

The sacred cat

In ancient Egypt, contented cats purred in Egyptian homes, wearing gold rings in their ears and noses. Cats were protected pets because many Egyptians worshiped them. There was even a law that a person who killed a cat could be punished by death.

When a favorite cat died, some people shaved off their eyebrows to show their sorrow and respect for their dead pet. They often mummified and then buried their cat in a cat-shaped coffin in the cemetery at Bubastis. Bubastis was the center of worship for the cat goddess, Bastet.

Egyptians no longer pray to many gods or Pharaohs, but religious **faith** is still a very important part of their everyday life. Today, the main religion in Egypt is Islam. Islam was introduced to the country in the 600s A.D., by Arabs, one of the many peoples who invaded Egypt throughout its history. Many Coptic Christians and a small number of Jews and Greek Orthodox Christians also live and worship in Egypt today.

Islam

The prophet Muhammad, who received and spread the teachings of *Allah*, founded the religion of Islam in 622 A.D. *Allah* is the Arabic name for God. People who follow Islam are known as Muslims. They pray to *Allah* five times a day: at dawn, at noon, in the afternoon, at nightfall, and in the evening. They also read from their holy book, the *Qur'an*.

Times of prayer

Five times a day, a crier, or *muezzin*, climbs a **minaret** and calls people to pray. When people hear the *muezzin*, they pray wherever they are. Some pray at home or at work, while others come to the **mosque**, a Muslim house of worship. Muslims face **Mecca** and often kneel on beautiful carpets to say their prayers. Mecca is the holy city in Saudi Arabia where Muhammad was born.

(above) Mosques, such as the Muhammad Ali Mosque, usually have roofs in the shape of a dome and tall towers called minarets.

*(right) A Muslim prays before a **mihrab**, a decorative alcove that shows Muslims in which direction to pray.*

Coptic Christianity

Christianity began in Israel over 2,000 years ago. Christians, or followers of Christianity, believe in one God. The religion of Christianity is based on the teachings of Jesus Christ, who is believed to be God's son on earth. In Egypt, most Christians belong to the Coptic Church. Copt is the Arabic name for the ancient Egyptians. Many Copts became Christian during the second century A.D. when Egypt was part of the Roman Empire. Copts make up about ten percent of Egypt's population.

The Coptic churches in Egypt are very old. Some of them are built in the shape of a cross. The cross has become a symbol of Christianity because Jesus Christ was **crucified**, or hung, on a cross. Other churches have rounded ceilings or domes. Most churches have beautiful wooden screens made of small beads that fit together like a puzzle. These screens separate the altar from the area where worshipers pray.

(above) A series of monasteries where Coptic monks could lead a peaceful life devoted to God were founded at Wadi Natrun around 400 A.D.

(below) Coptic women meet for a prayer group and Bible readings.

Music and dance

Music and dance have always played an important part in everyday Egyptian life. In ancient times, farmers sang work songs in the fields. Musicians played at public festivals. Dancing girls and orchestras of women performed at formal parties. Today, people who live in the city can go to the symphony one night and to a pop music concert the next. The **Bedouin** people of the desert, the **Nubians** from the south of Egypt, and the farmers who live along the Nile River have their own special dances and music.

Traditional musicians perform in a café. They are playing **mizmars**, *instruments that have a powerful sound similar to bagpipes.*

A menu of music

In Egypt today, you can listen to many different types of music. Classical Arabic music, which was written centuries ago, is still played on traditional instruments, such as the *oud* or *qanun*. *Al-musika al-shababeya* is a mixture of Arabic and European or North American music. Musicians play traditional Arabic instruments to a western beat. Many young Egyptians prefer their own pop music called *al jeel* or *el gil*. They like to dance to its fast and lively rhythms. Villagers and people who recently moved to the cities listen to *shaabi* music and dance *baladi*, or country, dances. Ahmed Adaweyah helped make *shaabi* popular. Today, *shaabi*'s traditional flute, stringed instruments, and drum sound is mixed with electronic beats.

Belly dancing

Belly dancing began many centuries ago. While a woman was giving birth, her closest female friends and relatives gathered around to encourage her. They rolled their hips in a way that showed the pregnant woman how to move so that she could speed up the birth. The pregnant woman copied their movements. In this way, the friends and relatives helped her give birth. Gradually, the movements became a dance.

Later, belly dancing became a form of entertainment. Belly dancers sway their hips and move their stomach muscles in time to the hypnotic beat of the *tabla* and *oud* music. In Egypt, brides and grooms often hire a belly dancer for their weddings. As the drums roll, the belly dancer leads the procession of wedding guests into the hall for the celebration. Most often, she balances a candelabra, or candleholder, on her head as she dances into the room. Sometimes, belly dancers use veils or swords as they perform their dances.

(above) Bedouin children dance in the desert just for fun!

(left) A belly dancer in a sparkling costume performs for tourists at a hotel.

Umm Kalthum

Umm Kalthum was one of the most popular classical singers in Egypt and throughout the Arab world. Her songs about love, Egypt, and Islam were sometimes more than an hour long! People never tired of hearing them, though. During her concerts, which would last for five hours, the audience would ask her to sing those songs over and over. When Umm Kalthum died in 1975, millions of people lined the streets of Cairo for her funeral. Her CDs and cassettes are still bestsellers, and there is a museum in Cairo dedicated to her memory.

Art

Egyptians have been creating art for thousands of years. In ancient times, they made delicate glassware and beautiful sculptures, jewelry, and pottery. They created colorful wall paintings on tombs and inside their homes that depicted scenes of daily life. Egyptians still make jewelry from gold or silver. They also handweave beautifully patterned carpets, called **kilims**, and create art to show their religious **devotion**.

Islamic art

Muslims believe that only *Allah* can create humans and animals. So, many artists do not show living creatures in their work, especially in religious buildings, such as mosques. Instead, they make complicated designs of leaves, flowers, vines, and abstract patterns. These designs are called **arabesques**. Muslim artists carve arabesque patterns in wood and stone, or paint them on tiles.

Calligraphy

Islam's holy book, the *Qur'an*, contains the exact words of *Allah*, and Muslims consider it to be sacred. The scribes who copy *Allah's* words honor him by trying to make their handwriting as beautiful as his ideas. This fine handwriting is called **calligraphy**. In Egypt, you will find calligraphy in many places besides books. Words from the *Qur'an* are carved on wood, stucco, and stone in mosques and monuments. Many Egyptian homes have paintings with *Allah's* name written in graceful script.

The walls and arched ceiling of a mosque are covered in intricate arabesques. Calligraphy, which runs just above the arches, displays words from the **Qur'an.**

The Children's Weaving Studio

Egypt has a long tradition of carpet and textile making. More than 50 years ago, an Egyptian architect, Wissa Wassef, and his wife, Sophie, an art teacher, founded a crafts school in Harraniya. Here, they taught children from the countryside how to use hand-driven **looms**, which are machines for weaving cloth. They encouraged the young weavers to create their own designs. The children made beautiful woven **tapestries** to hang on walls. The tapestries show birds, plants, and animals. Today, children at the school still prepare and spin their own wool. They use natural dyes made from vegetables to add color to their weavings. Visitors from all over the world come to Harraniya to buy these tapestries.

(above) A carpet maker weaves patterns on a loom.

(above) A carpet created by an artist trained at Wissa Wassef's art school shows life in an Egyptian village.

Arabic is Egypt's official language, but many Egyptians speak other languages as well. For example, the Siwan people, who live on the Siwa Oasis in the Western Desert, speak their own language. People who live in cities learn English and sometimes French in school. The Coptic language, similar to what ancient Egyptians spoke, is still used in the church services of Coptic Christians, even though it died out as a spoken language before the 1800s.

Forms of Arabic

There are three different forms of Arabic. Classical Arabic is the ancient language used in the *Qur'an*. Modern Arabic is used in formal writing and in schools. Egyptian Arabic is the language that people speak every day.

The Arabic alphabet has 28 letters. Arabic also uses a combination of dots to show vowel sounds. Words are written from right to left.

(above and below) A gym sign with Arabic script uses an illustration based on ancient art, and a store uses an Arabic and English sign.

Making movies

Arabs in different countries speak different **dialects**, or variations, of the same Arabic language. Many of them understand the Egyptian dialect because they watch so many Egyptian movies. Egypt's film industry used to be enormous, producing hundreds of films a year. Today, less films are made and there is more emphasis on television programs. Cairo is still called the "Hollywood of Arabia" and it is still home to the Cairo International Film Festival. The industry struggles with **censorship** inside the country and **piracy** outside the country. Film piracy costs the industry millions of dollars each year in lost ticket revenues.

Papers, books, and magazines

Egypt has a population of over 75 million and over 60 percent are **literate**. Egyptians are avid readers. The country has dozens of newspapers and magazines printed in Arabic and English. A small book publishing industry is supported by a yearly book fair in Cairo where publishers promote their books. Some publishers are offering books online, so that people all over the world can read Egyptian books.

A book stall display of Arabic language books.

Naguib Mahfouz

Naguib Mahfouz (1911-2006) was Egypt's most famous writer and author. When he was growing up in Cairo, there were no Egyptian novels. Instead, he read novels by European writers. Mahfouz began writing his own novels that captured the atmosphere of Old Cairo and of the city's people. His famous *Cairo Trilogy*, is a series of three books that traces the life of one family from 1919 to 1944. Mahfouz won the Nobel Prize for Literature in 1988.

Stories of gods and Pharaohs

Like people all over the world, Egyptians love stories. Through the ages, they have listened to myths and legends from ancient times. They have also enjoyed folk tales about everyday life. Here is one version of a legend from long ago.

The legend of Isis and Osiris

In the days when Egypt was still a young country, the god Osiris was the Pharaoh and the goddess Isis was the queen. They ruled the people wisely and well. But Osiris had a younger brother, Set, who was jealous and wanted the kingdom for his own.

One day when Isis was away, Set invited Osiris to a great feast. When the guests finished eating, Set brought in a beautiful chest covered with silver, gold, and precious stones. "Whoever fits into this chest shall keep it," he promised. One by one, the guests tried to lie down in the chest. Some were too tall and some were too short. When Osiris lay down, the fit was perfect. "Aha!" snarled Set, as he slammed the chest shut. Then, he filled all the cracks with lead and secretly sent the chest down the Nile River to sink.

When Isis found out what had happened, she went in search of Osiris's body. She knew he could not enter the kingdom of the dead until he had the proper funeral rites. Using her magical powers, Isis found Osiris's body and brought it home. Set flew into a jealous rage and tore Osiris's body into fourteen pieces. He scattered the pieces over the land of Egypt.

After giving birth to Horus, Osiris's son, Isis set out again. She traveled along the Nile in her papyrus boat, searching for the pieces of Osiris's body. She found thirteen pieces in thirteen different places. The fourteenth piece she never found. It was eaten by some fish in the Nile, who were cursed forever after.

Isis used her magic again to put Osiris's body back together. She did this thirteen times, one time for each piece that she found. Then, she buried the thirteen bodies where she found the different pieces. With each burial, there was a great funeral.

Once Osiris had his funerals, he was able to enter the land of Duat. There, he became king of the Underworld. When Horus grew up, he killed Set after many battles. The son of Osiris and Isis finally became the rightful Pharaoh of Egypt.

Glossary

Afterlife Life after death

amulet A small piece of jewelry worn as a charm against evil

arabesque A detailed design of leaves, flowers, and other shapes

Bedouin Arabs who live in the desert. Traditionally, they live in tents and move from place to place

calligraphy The art of beautiful handwriting

censorship Preventing people from seeing or hearing things

conqueror A person who gains control over a land by using force

Coptic An Egyptian language that is no longer widely used but is related to the language of the ancient Egyptians

crucify To put a person to death by nailing or tying to a cross

devotion Strong attachment, commitment, and dedication

dialect A particular form of a language spoken in one region

Egyptologist A person who studies the language, history, and culture of ancient Egypt

embalm To treat a dead body with chemicals so that it does not decay

faith Religious belief

hieroglyph A picture representing a word or sound used in ancient Egyptian writing

kilim A thin woven carpet made in the Middle East

kohl A black powder used as an eye makeup

limestone A rock used for building that is easy to carve

linen Cloth made from the fibers of the flax plant

literate Able to read

loom A device used to weave strands of thread together to produce cloth

Mecca The birthplace of the prophet Muhammad in Saudi Arabia, which is a holy place to followers of Islam

minaret A tall, slender tower from which a crier calls people to prayer

monument A structure built to remember a person or event

mosque A Muslim house of worship

natron A mineral form of salt

Nubian A person originally from southern Egypt or northern Sudan

papyrus A material on which to write, made from a tall water plant or the plant itself

Pharaoh A ruler of ancient Egypt

piracy Unauthorized use or copying

priest A religious leader

pyramid A building of ancient Egypt used as a burial place, with four sides shaped like triangles that meet in a point at the top

repatriate To bring something back to where it belongs

resin A sticky yellow or brown substance from some trees

scarab The sacred dung beetle of ancient Egypt

scribe A person who writes down the words of others, records information, or copies books, letters, and other kinds of writing

tapestry A heavy decorative weaving meant for hanging on walls

temple A building used for religious services

tomb A chamber or room for burying the dead

Underworld The imaginary place of the dead below the earth

worship To honor or respect a god

Index

Printed in the USA